PAULA ABDUL

A Real-Life Reader Biography

Susan Zannos

Mitchell Lane Publishers, Inc.
P.O. Box 200 • Childs, Maryland 21916

First Printing

Real-Life Reader Biographies

Selena	Robert Rodriguez	Mariah Carey	Rafael Palmeiro
Tommy Nuñez	Trent Dimas	Cristina Saralegui	Andres Galarraga
Oscar De La Hoya	Gloria Estefan	Jimmy Smits	Mary Joe Fernandez
Cesar Chavez	Chuck Norris	Sinbad	Paula Abdul
Vanessa Williams	Celine Dion	Mia Hamm	LeAnn Rimes

Library of Congress Cataloging-in-Publication Data
Zannos, Susan.
    Paula Abdul / Susan Zannos.
      p. cm. —(A real-life reader biography.)
    Includes Index.
    Summary: A brief biography of Paula Abdul, the talented and versatile dancer, choreographer, actress, and vocalist.
    ISBN 1-883845-74-2
    1. Abdul, Paula—Juvenile literature. 2. Singers—United States—Biography—Juvenile literature. 3. Dancers—United States—Biography—Juvenile literature. [1. Abdul, Paula. 2. Singers. 3. Dancers. 4. Entertainers. 5. Women—Biography.] I. Title. II. Series.
ML3930.A25Z36 1998
782.42166'092—dc21
[B]
                                          98-30669
                                               CIP
                                         AC MN

ABOUT THE AUTHOR: Susan Zannos has taught at all levels, from preschool to college, in Mexico, Greece, Italy, Russia, and Lithuania, as well as in the United States. She has published a mystery **Trust the Liar** (Walker and Co.) and **Human Types: Essence and the Enneagram** was published by Samuel Weiser in 1997. She has written several books for children, including **Paula Abdul** and **Cesar Chavez** (Mitchell Lane).

PHOTO CREDITS: cover: Shooting Star; p. 4 courtesy Bragman, Nyman, Cafarelli; p. 6 Laura D. Luongo/Shooting Star; p. 12 courtesy Bragman, Nyman, Cafarelli; p. 19 AP Photo/Mark Terrill; p. 24 Diana Lyn/Shooting Star; p. 26 Laura D. Luongo/Shooting Star; p. 27 Reuters/Corbis-Bettmann; p. 28 UPI/Corbis-Bettmann; p. 30 Ron Davis/Shooting Star.

ACKNOWLEDGMENTS: The following story has been thoroughly researched, and to the best of our knowledge, represents a true story. Though we try to authorize every story we publish, for various reasons, this is not always possible.

Table of Contents

Chapter 1
Valley Girl

Paula Abdul is a bundle of energy and creativity held together by a very special kind of genius. She's petite, barely 5 feet 2 inches tall, but her many talents and her hard work have made her an entertainment superstar.

Paula was born on June 19, 1963, in Los Angeles. Her mother is a Jewish French-Canadian; her father is Syrian and Brazilian.

"What am I? People ask me that all the time," Paula says. "I'm a

Paula's many talents and hard work have made her an entertain—ment superstar.

Valley girl, born and raised in the Valley." People who live in Los Angeles know that "the Valley" means the San Fernando Valley, a large area of middle-class neighborhoods between the mountains to the east and the hills along the Pacific Ocean. Paula grew up in an area called the Condos in Van Nuys, one of the Valley neighborhoods.

Paula (right) with her sister, Wendy

Paula's father, Harry, was a businessman. Her mother, Lorraine, had been a concert pianist and had a job in a movie studio. Paula also has a sister, Wendy, who is seven years older than she is. The whole family liked music and movies. They liked to watch musical films together.

Paula can remember watching movie star Gene Kelly dance in the movie *Singin' in the Rain.* She was only four years old, but she told her parents, "I want to do that!" Although she was too young to start dance lessons then, Paula tagged along to Wendy's lessons. Later, Paula would show her mother all the steps. Her mother remembers, "All you had to do was show her a move once, and she had it."

Paula started dance lessons when she was seven years old. At about that time, her parents were divorced. Paula loved both of her parents very much. The divorce was hard on her.

Paula kept very busy with her schoolwork and other activities. In fifth grade she sang in the school choir, was president of the square-

Paula was only four years old when she watched Gene Kelly dance in *Singin' in the Rain.*

dance club, and was on the speech and debate team. She also studied ballet, tap, jazz, and modern dance and performed with community theater groups. In the summers she performed with Young Americans, a traveling musical group.

When she went to Van Nuys Junior High School, Paula found that her light brown skin caused her problems. "There were Black gangs and Mexican gangs fighting each other," Paula remembers. "Blacks thought I was Mexican and Mexicans thought I was Black. I was caught in the middle. It was scary sometimes."

Paula's way of reacting to fear or any emotional pain was to work even harder. She was very athletic and played softball and basketball. In junior high school she was chosen to choreograph the school

Paula says, "Blacks thought I was Mexican and Mexicans thought I was Black."

play, *Hello Dolly*. Choreographing is planning the dances for a show. Paula's choreography was a big success.

By the time she got to Van Nuys High School, where such stars as Marilyn Monroe and Robert Redford had gone to school, hard work was a habit. In her senior year, this Valley girl played softball and basketball, played the flute in the school orchestra, was a member of the science team, was head cheerleader, and was chosen to be senior class president.

In junior high school, Paula was chosen to choreograph the school play.

Chapter 2
Laker Girl

People told Paula she couldn't be a dancer because she was too short.

When Paula Abdul graduated from high school, she wanted to go to college and study to be a sports announcer. People had told her that she couldn't be a dancer because she was too short. They said dancers had to be tall with long legs. Paula's body was short and rounded.

Years before, when Paula had first started dance classes, the teacher had talked about different types of bodies. The teacher wanted the children to understand that these differences were natural. She used Paula as an example of a short, rounded body. Paula was too young to understand. All she knew was that she was different. She didn't want to be different. She wanted to be tall and thin like her friends in dance class.

Thinking she could never be a dancer, Paula turned to her love of sports and decided to be a sports announcer. She started classes in radio and television at California State University at Northridge in 1981.

Going to college was expensive. Paula needed a part-time job to earn money. One of her friends told her that the Lakers, the famous Los Angeles basketball team, were having tryouts for the Laker Girls, the team's cheerleaders.

Thinking she could never be a dancer, Paula decided to be a sports announcer.

Paula had been head cheerleader when she was in high school. She thought that if she could be a Laker Girl, she would have a chance to meet the basketball players. She could talk to them and practice being a sports announcer. She thought the job would help her to earn some money and to prepare for her career. She was right about that, but not in the way she expected.

Paula went to the tryouts. When she got there she was shocked to see that there were hundreds of girls wanting to be Laker Girls. Most of them were tall and thin. Paula thought she didn't have a chance. Then she thought that since she had come, she might as well watch the other girls try out.

When it was Paula's turn, she decided she had nothing to lose by

Paula was head cheer– leader when she was in high school.

trying. She did the routine she had practiced. The judges liked it a lot. Paula was chosen to be a Laker Girl.

Paula started working with the other cheerleaders for the Lakers in 1982. When the woman in charge learned about Paula's dance background, she asked her for ideas for new cheers. Paula had lots of ideas. She mixed dance styles with the gymnastics and jumps that cheerleaders usually do.

The Laker Girls would do Paula's new dance routines before the games and at half time. The crowds who came to the basketball games enjoyed the new way the Laker Girls performed. Before long Paula was the head choreographer for the Laker Girls.

Because a part of Los Angeles, Hollywood, is home to the motion-picture and television industries,

Before long, Paula was the head choreo– grapher for the Laker Girls.

many Laker fans were in show business. Famous stars such as actor Jack Nicholson, talk show host Arsenio Hall, and the musical Jackson family came to Laker games. They liked to watch the Laker Girls, too. They liked the new routines that Paula Abdul created.

One night in 1984, after the Jacksons had been to a Laker Game, they decided they wanted Paula Abdul to fly to New York to choreograph a video they were making. Paula was shocked and afraid. She had never done anything like that before. She couldn't imagine telling famous stars like the Jacksons what to do. But even though she was afraid, she choreographed the video. It was the video for the song "Torture" from the Jacksons' *Victory* album.

One day, the Jacksons decided they wanted Paula to chore- ograph a video they were making.

Chapter 3
Choreographer

Suddenly, Paula was famous.

Suddenly Paula Abdul was famous. One day she was just an ordinary girl earning $50 a night as a cheerleader while going to college. Soon after, she was the most wanted choreographer in show business.

In 1985 Paula got a call from the A&M Record Company asking her to coach Janet Jackson on her dancing and to choreograph videos for her. Paula and Janet worked together for three hours every day.

Paula says, "Janet and I made each other look very good." Janet worked hard to learn the dance steps Paula taught her, and Paula worked hard to create dances that would make Janet Jackson's songs into flashy videos.

Paula Abdul's choreography combined many different kinds of movement into an exciting new style. She had taken lessons in tap dancing, ballet, jazz, and modern dance. From her cheerleading she knew gymnastics and jumps. And she knew the funky new dances that teenagers were doing.

She had so much work, she had to quit college and the Laker Girls.

Before long, Paula had so many jobs choreographing videos, television shows, and movies that she had to quit both her college studies and her job with the Laker Girls. Besides working with Janet Jackson and the Jackson brothers,

Sometimes, Paula dreams about a dance sequence and she writes it down later.

she choreographed videos for groups such as ZZ Top, Duran Duran, and the Pointer Sisters. She coached the movements of Eddie Murphy and Arsenio Hall in *Coming to America,* and of Arnold Schwarzenegger in *The Running Man.* She choreographed commercials and shows for television.

Paula says she creates her dances in different ways. Sometimes she will dream about a dance sequence, and when she wakes up she'll write down what she remembers. Sometimes she will work in a very small space, like her bathroom. In this way she gets ideas for close-ups because she can only see from the waist up in the bathroom mirror. Sometimes she works in very large spaces, like empty dance halls. There she can create the large movements the dancers will make.

Just as there are different steps that go into a dance, there are different steps that go into making a video of a dance. First, Paula gets the idea. Then she chooses the dancers and teaches them the movements. After the dance is rehearsed, the cameramen come and she tells them what types of shots to take.

Paula performed at Frank Sinatra's 80th birthday celebration.

Her choreo-graphy began winning awards.

Finally, when the film is developed, it is edited.

Editing film is taking the many images, or pictures, and fitting them together. It is a little like putting together a big puzzle. All the little images have to fit together so that the people watching believe they are seeing one complete action.

Before long, Paula Abdul's choreography began winning awards. In 1987 she won the American Video Arts Award for choreographer of the year. In 1989 she won an Emmy award for best choreography of a TV series for *The Tracey Ullman Show.* In 1990, she won MTV awards for best female video, best dance video, best choreography in a video, and best editing in a video, all for her own music video, "Straight Up."

Chapter 4
Entertainer

From the time four-year-old Paula had told her parents "I want to do that" while watching Hollywood musicals with her family, Paula Abdul wanted to be an all-around entertainer. She not only wanted to dance, she wanted to sing and to act as well. Even after she became a famous choreographer, she still wanted to show that she had other talents.

Paula had been in a musical group in high school, so she had some background in singing. One

Paula wanted to show that she had other talents as well.

day, when she was choreographing a video for another singer, she went up to one of the men from the record company and told him she wanted to make records. The man agreed to help her.

Even after she had signed a contract to make a recording, she kept her singing career a secret. Many people who knew her and worked with her were completely surprised when her first album, *Forever Your Girl*, was released in June of 1988.

One of the biggest hits from that album, "Straight Up," became the number one song in the country. Other singles such as "Knocked Out" and "The Way That You Love Me" also became big hits. The album sold 12 million copies, making Paula Abdul a singing

Her first album, *Forever Your Girl*, was released in 1988.

superstar even before she made the music videos for her songs.

Paula was already famous as a choreographer. When her records became hits, she was famous all over the world as a singer. She went on concert tours not only in the United States but in England and other European countries as well. The video "Under My Spell" was made at one of her sold-out concerts in Japan.

Paula's next album, *Spellbound,* came out in 1991 and also hit the top of the popular music charts. Her music videos, now with Paula choreographing and dancing to her own songs, continued to win awards. Her singing also was winning awards. In 1990 she won American Music Awards for favorite dance artist and favorite

Soon, she won awards for her singing as well.

pop-rock female. That same year she won the People's Choice Award for favorite female musical performer.

Paula in a diet Coke commercial.

After her huge success as a singer, Paula wanted to be an actress. Her first acting roles were on the television shows *Cybill* and *The Single Guy*. After these experiences, Paula said, "I've really got the acting bug now. . . . It's definitely something I want to focus on. I always wanted to be an all-around entertainer." In January of 1997, she starred in the ABC Sunday Night Movie *Touched by Evil.*

Chapter 5
Balance

Paula Abdul seemed to have everything. She was famous as a choreographer and dancer. She was famous as a singer and had many hit songs. And she had started her acting career. She was a superstar.

Paula was no longer a Valley girl. She had a $3 million home in Beverly Hills. She could buy all the beautiful clothes she wanted. Most people thought her life was perfect. But it wasn't.

Paula had a big problem, which she tried to keep secret. It

Most people thought her life was perfect. But it wasn't.

was a disease called bulimia. People who have bulimia cannot control their eating. Instead of eating a healthy diet, they eat too much and they eat the wrong kinds of food. Then, because they don't want to be fat, they go into a bathroom and make themselves throw up.

Paula performed at the 1997 AIDS Dance-A-Thon.

When Paula had started to get famous, she was working very hard. At one point, when her singing career was just beginning, she was very busy. Her schedule would begin in the morning, when she would choreograph *The Tracey Ullman Show* for television. This lasted until two o'clock in the afternoon. After that she would rehearse George Michael for his tour. Then, from seven until ten o'clock at night, she would work with the dancers for the movie *Coming to America.* After that she would go to the recording studio to record her album. She would stay until four in the morning.

Sometimes she didn't even have time to eat. She would get very hungry—so hungry that when she finally did eat, she would eat too much. Then she would feel bad and make herself throw up. She knew that she shouldn't do this, but she was

Paula and husband Emilio Estevez arrive at a benefit premiere of the film Sleepless in Seattle.

afraid of getting fat. The more famous Paula became, the more fear she felt. She thought that she had to be perfect, and she thought that being perfect meant being thin. The harder she tried, it seemed, the more her eating habits got out of control.

There were other problems, too. In 1992 she married actor Emilio Estevez, but two years later the marriage ended in divorce. Also at that time, one of her backup singers, Yvette Marine, claimed it was her voice, not Paula's, on Paula's record. The record company proved that Paula did her own singing, but Paula was very upset over the incident.

Paula responded publicly to accusations by a backup singer that she sang lead vocals on Paula's album.

Finally, after filing for divorce in 1994, Paula went to a private clinic that treated eating problems. She was still trying to keep her bulimia a secret, but some photographers saw her. They sold pictures of Paula at the clinic to newspapers. Her problem became front page news.

At the clinic, Paula learned good habits to replace her bad habits. Now she is guided by her three most important rules: Eat three balanced meals a day instead of skipping meals. Exercise only one hour a day instead of hours and hours in an effort to stay thin. And most important, accept the size and shape she was born with instead of wishing she were tall and thin.

Paula's life became more balanced. She understands that she

In 1994, Paula went to a private clinic that treated eating problems.

Paula, with second husband, Brad Beckerman.

can't hide her feelings by working too hard and too long.

In 1995, Paula met clothing designer Brad Beckerman on a blind date. They fell in love, and in November 1996 they were married in a fairy-tale wedding. Her whole family and many, many friends were there. Even though this marriage ended in 1998, Paula feels more sure of herself now. She takes more time for the people she loves.

Paula Abdul, who became famous as a choreographer, a dancer, a singer, and an actress, is now also enjoying her success at the most important art: living a balanced life.

Discography

Selected Top Singles

"Straight Up" (1988)
"Forever Your Girl" (1988)
"Cold Hearted" (1988)
"The Way That You Love Me" (1988)
"Opposites Attract" (1988)
"Rush Rush" (1991)
"The Promise of a New Day" (1991)
"Vibeology" (1991)
"My Love Is for Real" (1995)
"Ain't Never Gonna Give You Up" (1995)
"Crazy Cool" (1995)

Albums

Forever Your Girl (1988)
Shut Up and Dance: The Dance Mixes (1990)
Spellbound (1991)
Head Over Heels (1995)

Videos

Straight Up: The Videos (1989)
Captivated: The Video Collection '92 (1992)
Under My Spell Tour Live (1993)
Get Up and Dance (An Aerobic Dance Workout) (1995)

Chronology

- 1963, born June 19 in Los Angeles, California
- 1970, began dance lessons
- 1981, started studying at California State University at Northridge
- 1982, began cheerleading and choreographing for the Laker Girls
- 1986, left Laker Girls to concentrate on her choreography career
- 1987, won American Video Arts Award for choreographer of the year
- 1988, hit album *Forever Your Girl* released in June
- 1989, won Emmy award for best choreography for *The Tracey Ullman Show*; won MTV awards for best female video, best dance video, best choreography in a video, and best editing in a video for "Straight Up"
- 1991, album *Spellbound* released; sued by backup singer Yvette Marine
- 1992, married Emilio Estevez on April 29
- 1994, divorced Emilio Estevez
- 1996, married clothing designer Brad Beckerman in November
- 1997, starred in television movie *Touched by Evil*
- 1998, ended marriage to Brad Beckerman

Index